# Practical
# PRAYING

# Also by John Edward

## BOOKS

*AFTER LIFE: Answers from the Other Side* (with Natasha Stoynoff)

*CROSSING OVER: The Stories Behind the Stories*

*FINAL BEGINNINGS* (a novel), co-authored with Natasha Stoynoff

*ONE LAST TIME: A Psychic Medium Speaks to Those We've Loved and Lost*

*WHAT IF GOD WERE THE SUN?* (a novel)*

## AUDIO PROGRAMS

*CROSSING OVER: The Stories Behind the Stories* (audio book)

*DEVELOPING YOUR OWN PSYCHIC POWERS* *

*UNDERSTANDING YOUR ANGELS AND MEETING YOUR GUIDES* *

*UNLEASHING YOUR PSYCHIC POTENTIAL* *

*WHAT IF GOD WERE THE SUN?* (audio book)*

*Also in Spanish

All of the above are available at your local bookstore, or may be
ordered by visiting any of the following distributors for Princess books:
Hay House USA: **www.hayhouse.com**
Hay House Australia: **www.hayhouse.com.au**
Hay House UK: **www.hayhouse.co.uk**
Hay House South Africa: **orders@psdprom.co.za**

# Practical PRAYING

## Using the Rosary to Enhance Your Life

John Edward

Princess Books
New York, NY.

*To my cousin Josephine ("jo jo"):*

*Thank you for helping me to rediscover
the Magic of Christmas*

# Contents

*Introduction:* Do You Pray?                                    ix

**Chapter 1:**   Who, Me?
               Write about the Rosary?        1

**Chapter 2:**   My Own Journey                 25

**Chapter 3:**   Using the Rosary:
               The Official Way               63

**Chapter 4:**   Practical Praying:
               Creating Your Story            79

*References*                                  101

*About the Author*                            103

## Introduction

# *Do You Pray?*

*Prayer is universal in design,
but personal in definition.*

P rayer.
It's something we all do, even those of us who may
not especially think that we believe in God or a Higher
Power. Think about it . . . how many times in the course of a
week, a day, or even a single hour do you say the words, "Oh
God," or "God help me"? You may not think this is praying,
but in a very fundamental way, it *is* prayer in its most basic
form—a plea or call to God for help, assistance, or guidance.

Like millions of people in this world, I use prayer every
day of my life. It centers me, rejuvenates me, and puts me in
touch with the universe and its maker. It has opened, and

continues to open, my spirit and soul to the infinite power and possibilities of the life energy that connects us all.

This is a book about how I came to embrace the power of prayer in a very practical way, thus the title, *Practical Praying*. Specifically, I will discuss and share with you my personal method of praying, using meditation and the Rosary. They have enhanced my life immeasurably, and it is my sincere hope that they will do the same for you.

Before we begin, I'd like you to look at a few definitions that I'll refer back to throughout the following pages. Read them over once or twice to become familiar with them, and then we'll begin a new, exciting, and potentially life-changing adventure together.

**Meditation:** Private religious devotion or mental exercise, in which techniques of concentration and contemplation are used to reach a heightened level of spiritual awareness. The practice has existed in all religions since ancient times. In Hinduism it has been systematized in the school of Yoga. One aspect of Yoga, dhyana (*Sanskrit:* "Concentrated meditation"), gave rise to a school of its own among the Buddhists, becoming the basis of Zen. In many religions, meditation involves verbal or mental repetition of a single syllable, word, or text (e.g., a mantra).

Visual images (e.g., a mandala) or mechanical devices such as prayer wheels or rosaries can be useful in focusing concentration. In the 20th century, movements such as Transcendental Meditation emerged to teach meditation techniques outside a religious context.[1]

**Rosary:** [Rose garden], prayer of Roman Catholics, in which beads are used as counters. The term, applied also to the beads, is extended to Muslim, Hindu, and Buddhist prayers that use beads. The traditional Catholic Rosary is a series of 15 meditations on events (mysteries) in the lives of Jesus and Mary. The joyful mysteries are the Annunciation, the Visitation, the birth of Jesus, his presentation at the Temple, and the finding of the child Jesus among the doctors. The sorrowful mysteries are the agony of Jesus in the garden, his scourging, the crowning with thorns, the carrying of the Cross, and the Crucifixion. The glorious mysteries are the Resurrection, the Ascension, the descent of the Holy Ghost, the assumption of The Virgin, and her coronation as Queen of Heaven.

In 2002, Pope John Paul II proposed the addition of five "mysteries of light" drawn from Jesus' public life: his baptism in the Jordan, his self-manifestation at the wedding at Cana, his proclamation of the kingdom of God, the Transfiguration, and his institution of the Eucharist. As one dwells on a mystery in thought, one recites prayers—the Lord's Prayer (or Our Father; Paternoster) once, Hail Mary (Ave Maria) ten times, and Glory Be to the Father (Gloria Patri) once. Count is kept by slipping beads through the fingers; the beads have no other significance. The usual string—formerly called the chaplet—has five sets of ten beads (decades); between the decades a single bead is set apart, for the Glory of one mystery and the Our Father of the next. There is a pendant with crucifix and beads for introductory prayers. The Rosary is often said in common, but it remains an individual prayer. Its popularity is often ascribed to the combination of simplicity of method with solidity of subject matter. In one form or another, it has been in use some 600 years.[2]

**Prayer:** The act of attempting to verbally [or silently] communicate with the supernatural. It's sometimes communal, as during a church service; it's sometimes done in private. Its purpose within Christianity is to assess the will of God for one's life, to praise God, to give thanks to God, to repent of sinful behavior, to ask forgiveness, to seek a favor from God, and (occasionally) to ask God to curse an opponent. Prayer is found in almost all religions.[3]

# Chapter One

# *Who, Me?*
# *Write about*
# *the Rosary?*

It's 7 P.M.—just one hour
before I'll walk onstage in
front of 10,000 people, most
of whom are desperate for me
to connect them with their
departed loved ones. I need to
calm myself, focus my energy,
and open myself up spiritually
to the Other Side.

Alone in my hotel room, I
pick up my Rosary and silently
begin to pray. *I'm praying this
decade for the audience to learn
that their loved ones are still
with them. . . . I'm praying this*

*decade for me to be a clear receiver for them tonight. . . . I'm praying this decade for the energies to communicate with me in ways I will understand. . . .*

The beads slip through my fingers as I pray with intention—envisioning that I'll be the best teacher I can possibly be when I step into the spotlight and begin taking questions.

When I'm finished—it usually takes me about 30 minutes—I'm centered, focused, and tuned in to the Other Side. I'm ready to go to work.

Using a Rosary to pray is a ritual I've performed before every reading, seminar, or group session in my 20 years as a psychic medium. Oh, the method varies from day to day, depending on where I am and how much time I have. Sometimes I'll pray in the shower, when I'm racing to an engagement, while waiting backstage, in the car, or in an elevator using my compact "credit card" Rosary that I keep in my wallet. If I don't have a Rosary with me—which isn't very often—I simply use my fingers to pray. The point is, I always pray: every day, every night, and before every event.

Whatever my method, the result is always the same: Praying the Rosary opens me spiritually, helps me connect with my spirit guides, and allows me to conduct my own "dialogue" with God whenever and wherever I want.

Anyone who knows me is aware that my Rosary is like my American Express card—I won't leave home without it. I own at least a dozen, and they're all well worn—because I use them before I step on a plane, if a friend is having problems, and when someone I care about is ill. There's one in my briefcase, one in the glove compartment of my car, and there's even one hanging near my son's crib in his nursery.

As many others who pray the Rosary have discovered, having one can be like carrying a cell phone that connects us directly to Heaven—and that's a call you always want to make.

But why should I, a psychic medium, be talking to you about prayer and the Rosary? That's the question I asked myself repeatedly during the past two years as I started, stopped, and restarted the writing of this book.

Over the years, I've become known for my openness when it comes to my work as a psychic medium and teacher. If you've ever seen me at a seminar or on TV, or read any of my books, you know all too well that I never shy away from using very personal examples from my life to illustrate or communicate the messages I'm trying to get across. I've revealed some of the most intimate and personal moments of my family's joys and sorrows—not an easy thing for anyone to do, even among trusted friends—and I've always done it on a stage in front of thousands of people I've never even met.

But writing about prayer and the Rosary, which is what this book is all about, has proven to be the most difficult task I've ever attempted. During one of my many moments of procrastination during this project, my friend Jon asked why

I was having such difficulty. Only while trying to answer his question did I realize why I'd developed such a bad case of writer's block—in fact, the answer became crystal clear: Prayer is *so* personal and *so* private to me that it's never been a subject I've felt comfortable talking about in public. What's that old adage—*never* discuss politics or religion at social functions? So I decided that in order to complete this book, I was going to have to sit down and write out my thoughts as though I were talking to a close friend.

So, *friend*, it's with you in mind that I complete this assignment. I truly hope that it inspires you.

## An Ancient Tool

Why should I embrace the concept of praying the Rosary? I'm sure that many of you reading this right now—especially the non-Catholics among you—are wondering the same thing and asking that same question. It's clearly a concept synonymous to, and identifiable with, one religion: Catholicism. And, as I've said many times in my books and lectures, I believe that no religion is the "right" one, but that each is like an airplane all taking us to the same destination. Each airline may have a different name and a different route, but all will take us to the same place in the end.

My dearest friend, psychic Shelley Peck, used to use the Rosary as a method of meditation. She even had a beautiful Rosary bracelet made for herself, which may not seem so odd . . . until you realize that Shelley was Jewish! I gave her a lot of credit for being public about using a Rosary because she came under a lot of criticism from fellow Jews for it. I still laugh out loud when I think of her response once when a Jew asked her why she carried the Rosary. She replied, "Because it would be a bitch to carry a menorah in my purse!" Shelley and I both saw religions as different languages to communicate with God.

As you've seen in the previous definitions of the words *meditation, Rosary,* and *prayer,* counting beads has been used as a tool in praying for centuries, and has been adopted in many different cultures and religions. For me, the Rosary is just that—a tool, a focal point, and a telephone of sorts—which helps me start what I refer to as a "Prayer Dialogue" with God. But before we go any further on our journey together, I want to make a couple of things perfectly clear: I'm *not* on the Vatican's payroll, and I'm definitely *not* looking to convert people from *their* religion or belief system to Catholicism.

The only goal I hope to achieve by writing this book is to share my personal experiences and beliefs about the power of prayer, and how I think it can be used to assist you in your everyday life. In the end, I believe that it really doesn't matter *how* you pray, as long as you *are* praying!

There are so many religions in the world and so many methods of praying, and I'm choosing to use the Rosary as the center of this discussion because it's how *I* like to pray— it's my own way of talking to God. In the same way that you'd choose a cellular-phone carrier to communicate with the people in your life, praying the Rosary is like choosing a "carrier" to facilitate the Prayer Dialogue with God . . . and the good news is that your "calling plan" isn't limited to evenings and weekends—it's boundless and infinite.

## But . . . Why Not Just Talk to God?

One evening over dinner in Miami not too long ago, I had a discussion about this book with my friend, actress Lucie Arnaz. She posed the exact same question so many people seem to have about using the Rosary: "Why not just pray?" she asked. "Why not just talk out loud and have a dialogue? Aren't you limiting people's options by saying that using the Rosary is the way to pray?"

No! That's just the thing—when it comes to prayer, there *are* no limits. One of my favorite movies is *The Matrix,* a film starring Keanu Reeves as a computer hacker who discovers that the world he's living in is just a virtual-reality façade. Keanu's character has to bend a spoon with his mind. It's an impossible task, until he realizes that the material world he's always believed he's lived in is, in reality, just a made-up computer fantasy. Once he truly recognizes and accepts that truth, he can bend the spoon . . . in fact, he can do nearly anything. That's where the film's classic line comes from ("There is no spoon"), meaning that when we truly believe—when we remove the blinders from our eyes—there are *no limits;* we're free to become who we're truly meant to be.

That's how I feel about life in general. And I believe that the power of prayer can help liberate our true potential; that once we embrace a personal Prayer Dialogue to connect with God, all the possibilities of life open up to us in their limitless glory. Praying helps us get to that level, so again, it doesn't matter *how* you start praying—just start!

During one of my seminars in Australia, someone in the audience asked me a question about religion. As I said earlier, I normally don't discuss the concepts behind any religion. The reason is simple: I'm Catholic and don't want my message to be tuned out by anyone because they're *not* Catholic. Religious denomination shouldn't really matter. Besides, as a psychic medium, I've always felt that I'm painting a "portrait of energy"—a process that's more scientific in theory than it is religious. For me, the religious aspect of my work lies in framing the energy portrait—every person can, and should, frame their own individual view of spiritual energy in whatever way suits them best.

But back to this one particular night in Australia. As soon as the audience member asked me about religion and God, the "Boys" (what I call my spirit guides) came through and defined God to me as a pyramid. They described each side of the "God pyramid" as having its own color, all symbolically representing a different religion. One side was blue, another green, another red, and the last side was orange. For those who see the blue side, they believe God is blue on *all* sides, and they call God blue; for those who can only see the green side, all sides *must be* green, and they call God green; and the same holds true for the red and orange sides. Each person (or group) is looking at the God pyramid from their own perspective—from their own side. They tend to believe that *their* color/religion/God is the only true one. But, in actuality, God is *all sides, all colors,* and multifaceted in His/Her energy. It's a remarkable way of looking at God, and when I delivered the Boys' description of the God pyramid to the audience that night—actually hearing it for the first time myself as it came out of my mouth—I was truly in awe of the definition.

For the longest time, I've always felt that all world religions contain some truths within them. I only wish that most creeds would embrace and teach what my guides described—that we're all looking at the same God, just from a different vantage point. If that was the way religious doctrine was taught, maybe, just maybe, people would lose their myopic views and stop fighting wars in the "name of God."

I feel that it's important to disclose here that I'm not a theologian, minister, priest, reverend, deacon, or, quite honestly, an authority on *any* religion—even Catholicism. To tell you the truth, I was actually thrown out of Catholic religion classes on two different occasions when I was younger. When my mom asked Church officials why I'd been dismissed, she was told that I was asking too many "challenging" questions and making others doubt their faith. I guess I've never taken things— especially things dealing with spirituality—at face value, or simply accepted certain ideas just because someone told me they had "the answer" or "one true way" of believing.

By writing this book, I'm not trying to make you doubt or question your faith, and I'm definitely not trying to start up any kind of organized religion or convert others to Catholicism— I'm just laying out a method of praying that's always worked for me. Honestly, you could read this whole book, learn about the Rosary, and decide that it just doesn't resonate with you as a prayer tool. That's all right. I still hope that you continue to pray in your own way, and hopefully incorporate some of the methods of practical praying into your own prayer sessions and experience the Prayer Dialogue that has worked so well for me. I just want to share my philosophy and personal experiences with prayer and its energy with you, my friend, so that you can begin operating on another level, and take your life, and the lessons it has to offer you, to the next plane.

Always remember: Believe . . . create . . . achieve!

# Oh God! (If God Calls, Will You Answer?)

I have a confession to make—it wasn't my idea to write this book. All the credit for that goes to my spirit guides, the Boys, who directed me toward the subject matter and then inspired me to put it into words.

Let me explain how this all came about. When my second nonfiction book, *Crossing Over: The Stories Behind the Stories,* was published in Australia, I traveled there on a lecture tour to help promote it. One afternoon while sitting on the balcony of my hotel overlooking the Sydney harbor, my spirit guides came through with a message that took me completely by surprise. And I responded to them out loud: "What?! I need to write a book about the Rosary?"

My mind instantly zoomed ahead to the conversation I'd need to have with my publisher to get approval to write such a book. I laughed nervously at the thought, and then imagined how the conversation might go:

**Me:** "I think I'm supposed to write a book about the Rosary and prayer."

**Publisher:** *"Nooooooooooooooooooo!"*

As I looked down from the hotel balcony and watched the hundreds of people below scurrying through their daily lives, rushing to and from the Sydney Opera House, clambering in and out of water taxis, and swarming the shops in the small, densely populated area surrounding the building known as the "Toaster," I pondered the message I'd received from the Boys. After a moment of quiet contemplation, I asked (again, out loud), "Are you guys sure?"

At that precise moment, the phone in my room rang. It was the president of Hay House (my publisher), Reid Tracy, who was traveling with me on the book tour, asking if he could stop by my room for a moment. I told him to come on by, and I immediately started trying to figure out how to tell him what my spirit guides had just told me to do. I was sure that he'd say it was a crazy idea, and I actually decided to put off telling him about it until after the trip. I even toyed with the notion of blowing the whole thing off entirely and using my free will to "take a pass" on the guides' suggestion. I'd never, *ever* had a conversation with Reid—who is not only my publisher, but also my friend—about religion, prayer, or God. I had no idea where he weighed in on any of this, and honestly, I still don't. But a very strange thing happened after he arrived in my room.

We sat there for a few minutes exchanging small talk—the weather, how the tour was going, if I was enjoying Australia, and so on. Then the conversation suddenly turned to publishing, and he wanted to know if we could talk about my thoughts on future books. I was a bit surprised by the question because I was already in the middle of writing a book called *After Life: Answers from the Other Side*. I wondered if this was the Boys giving me a cue: Was this the time to bring up their message? Reid continued chatting, saying that he felt I should be writing on a specific topic. I prepared myself, expecting him to suggest something really New-Agey—but instead, he looked at me and blurted out, "John, I think your next book should be about the Rosary!"

I was so stunned that I had to ask him to repeat what he'd just said. He did, but I still couldn't believe my ears and asked him to repeat it a second time. When he said I should write my next book on the Rosary for the *third* time, it finally hit home: It was the validation I guess I needed to hear. Sometimes even a psychic needs to be hit over the head a few times to get the message.

Why did Reid feel so strongly about my writing this book? I guess because during the many times he's heard me lecture to groups of thousands of people, he started to realize that one of the most frequent questions I'm asked is how I prepare for my sessions. And my answer has always been the same: I meditate by praying the Rosary.

Even with my publisher wholeheartedly on board for a book on the Rosary, I was nevertheless reluctant to follow the message from my spirit guides. I still had some issues to deal with. For example, I remembered that every time this TV producer I'd worked with early on in my career booked me on one of his shows, he'd always ask me the same question:

Had I ever seen the 1977 film *Oh, God!*? Sure, I'd seen the old favorite starring George Burns and John Denver on TV, but it certainly hadn't impressed me enough to earn a spot in my pop-culture-obsessed heart.

I finally asked the producer to elaborate, and he told me that I reminded him of the John Denver character, Jerry Landers—an assistant manager at a Los Angeles supermarket whom God has chosen to be his spokesperson on Earth. God wants Jerry to tell humankind that they've made a mess of the world, but that it's within their power to fix things. Jerry's sure that everyone will be convinced he's crazy for believing he can talk to the Almighty, and he's very reluctant to carry out God's wishes.

In an uncanny way, I now look at the producer's statement as a prediction. Not in regards to my psychic mediumship—I've always embraced my abilities and have never been reluctant when it came to carrying out my work as a teacher—but when it comes to writing this book, well, let's just say the producer's prediction came eerily true. Like John Denver's character, I was getting a loud and clear message from a Higher Source to do something, but I couldn't bring myself to do it!

Whenever I sat down at my computer to work on this book, I'm embarrassed to admit, I found every reason under the sun to distract myself. I procrastinated in good Libran fashion while continually asking my spirit guides, "Are you sure about this? Why me?"

They *were* sure, and their answer was simple and direct: "To help those who read the book start a Prayer Dialogue in their own lives."

I want to be absolutely clear here: I don't feel that I've in any way been "chosen," or that God Himself has appointed me to this position. But I do know that in the universal scheme of things, writing this book is something I'm supposed to be doing. It's the next step in my journey as a teacher, and the next path I must follow in my own personal and professional growth. I view it like this: We're all students in the same class, and I happened to have found a study method that has yielded some very positive results. Now all I'm doing is just helping my fellow students understand the way I achieved my goals and how they can as well. No great mystery.

As I've already said, I've always felt—and still do—that prayer is a very private and personal matter. It's not something I readily discuss, even with my family and friends, so the prospect of writing a book about it was very uncomfortable for me. But after 20 years of unconditionally accepting the guidance I've received from the Boys, I realized that I had no choice but to write this to help inspire others. My way of teaching is to share my personal thoughts and experiences with you. By doing so, maybe I'll encourage you to make prayer a part of your daily life. That alone will make my internal struggle while writing this book more than worthwhile!

## The Catholic Question

When I tell people that I prepare for my sessions by meditating and praying the Rosary, it generally leads to the inevitable question: "How do you reconcile doing the type of work you do with being a Catholic? Don't mediumship and all things psychic go against the Church?"

Well, the answer is, even in a strictly black-and-white interpretation of Church doctrine and the Bible, it would depend on who in the Church is doing the interpreting. For the most part, the men and women of the cloth have been extremely supportive of my work and the messages I receive regarding the afterlife. It's usually those I refer to as "holy rollers" who take the most offense at what I do.

A good example of this can be found in something that happened during one of the early tapings of the TV show I hosted called *Crossing Over with John Edward*. I was answering questions from the studio audience and pointed to a woman who had her hand up. But instead of asking me a question, she began riddling me with chapter-and-verse quotations from the Bible. She didn't have any questions at all; her only interest was in criticizing me and my work. The rest of the audience—who were all there hoping to connect with their loved ones on the Other Side—were getting irate. They weren't interested in her biblical tirade or listening to her as she tried to "save" me. Eventually they turned their anger toward *her,* but I quieted them down and asked her to continue.

When she was done, I asked her how the Bible was written.

"It was written by God," she answered.

"Did God himself put ink to parchment?" I challenged her.

She was ready with her answer, piping up with, "God wrote the Bible in the hearts of man for all to read."

I smiled at her and agreed. Then I asked, "How does God speak to the hearts of man for all to read?"

She answered, "God *inspired* man with His messages and thoughts."

Again, I agreed. *Inspired,* I pointed out, was a derivative of the word *inspiration,* which comes from the Latin, meaning, "in or of the spirit."

By arguing her case, she'd validated mine—God inspires all of us, myself included. We shouldn't let ourselves be limited by an overly strict interpretation of the Bible or any other religious book. As Shakespeare's Hamlet, after speaking with his father's ghost, says to his disbelieving friend: "There are more things in heaven and earth, Horatio, than are dreamt of in your philosophy."

But still, many people have a hard time trying to fit their expansive spiritual beliefs into the religious framework they were raised in. I totally understand that. Many people who are familiar with my first book, *One Last Time,* will know that I shared the readings I'd done for a Catholic nun and priest. (The priest, whom I called Father Patrick Moran [a pseudonym], has since become one of my dearest friends, and someone with whom I discuss all things religious and spiritual.) At that time in my life and career, I was convinced that my work and spiritual beliefs were not, and never would be, accepted or recognized by the Church. I felt completely isolated from my religion, as though I'd been excommunicated. I was having what you might call a crisis of faith.

But then, on a single summer day, God sent two of his many Earthly messengers to see me—and they've had an amazing impact on my life.

Father Patrick and a nun I'll call Sister Frances were from different cities and were complete strangers to each other—but they'd both booked separate appointments for readings with me on the same day. And both were on a mission to "check me out" after learning that some of their parishioners had been to see me to connect with their loved ones on the Other Side. The sessions had helped their parishioners, but they still wanted to see me with their own eyes to make sure I was legitimate.

Both Father Patrick and Sister Frances were kind, generous, and open-minded. When I did individual readings for them, each one experienced the process of connecting with loved ones who'd crossed over, and each saw how that "spiritual" experience can profoundly help a grieving person's healing process. I was able to connect both of them with some of their relatives in very meaningful and fulfilling readings—providing specific details and names that resonated with them and which validated the process.

After their readings, I discussed with each of them how I felt my work, faith, and beliefs were all really in the Divine light of God. Both of them thought that my work brought me closer to God, and they encouraged me to continue. Father Patrick and Sister Frances helped me confirm what I'd believed all along: that I'm simply acting as an instrument for God, to play in his own personal orchestra.

I don't think it's a coincidence that two separate people from different cities—and both of whom were members of the clergy—came to see me on the same day, and at a time when I felt abandoned by the Church and on the verge of abandoning my faith. They'd come to "investigate" whether I was taking advantage of their parishioners' faith, but ended up "investing" their faith in me. By connecting *them* to their relatives, they helped *me* remain connected to God. That day, God threw me a spiritual life preserver at a time when I truly needed His help.

Almost 18 years later, I booked a trip to the Caribbean specifically to get away and focus on writing this book. I was still dragging my feet a little . . . all right, all right, I was dragging them a lot. (Are you seeing a theme here?) As I stared at my blank computer screen, the phone rang at the house I'd rented, and my assistant patched through Father Patrick.

"John, how's that book on the Rosary coming along?"

*Aaaaaaaaagggggghhhh!* Pardon the intended pun here, but I *confessed* to him that I was really in a quandary over this book. I admitted that I was afraid I was really going to get creamed for writing it. His response was as pure and direct as the one he'd given me 18 years earlier.

"Stop worrying, John. You won't be writing this book alone—you'll have many spiritual helpers. The book is like every other aspect of your work, and it's absolutely necessary. So many people need it to help them find their way on their life path. You've been given a voice . . . use it. Now stop worrying and start writing. Get to work!"

Father Patrick told me to think about the many people who come to me, hoping that I can help connect them with their loved ones on the Other Side. He reminded me that when I'm helping people connect with those who have passed, I'm really acting as a conduit, a medium, and a teacher.

"John, this book is really no different from what you've been doing all along," he said. "You'll still be acting as a conduit, a medium, and a teacher. You've taught people by using your abilities as a medium to connect them with their loved ones who've passed. But this time your task will be to teach and inspire people by showing them how to connect directly with God. So start writing the book, and then just step out of the way. Just be yourself, the John that everyone knows—share your thoughts and beliefs, and let God take care of the rest. After all, this is really His book, not yours!"

I laughed out loud and retorted, "Well, then, can I put God's name on it?"

Father Patrick didn't laugh. He just said, "His name already *is* on it . . . He just doesn't care about getting any credit."

Most acknowledgments get written either in the front or back of a book, but I want to write a special thank-you to Father Patrick right here. That phone call came at a pivotal moment for me, as his presence in my life had years earlier. I believe in the theory that nothing happens by accident, and maybe this book will be like an unexpected, but much-needed, phone call for *you*.

## The First Attack

Even if this book does act as a spiritual wake-up call for you, the question is: Will you pick up the phone? Before I'd even finished Chapter 1, I realized the kind of resistance I was going to run into from those with narrow minds.

I'd just begun the writing process when I came down with a severe viral infection and needed a battery of tests to make sure it wasn't an appendix or gallbladder problem. Because I'd worked at a Long Island hospital for many years, I decided to go there for the tests and take the opportunity to visit some old friends who still worked there. One of them is my good buddy Kathy Barnaby, one of my favorite people in the world, whom I've known since I was 20 years old. We greeted each other warmly, and soon I was telling her about the prayer book I'd started. She loved the idea. Kathy was raised Catholic, but is very open and has a strong spiritual overlay to her basic Catholic beliefs.

As we were chatting, one of Kathy's co-workers came into the office to pick up paperwork. I had no idea who she was, but she clearly knew me and wasn't shy about jumping into our conversation. "If you don't mind me asking, where do your so-called messages and visions come from?" she demanded, reminding me of the woman at that early taping of *Crossing Over*.

Again, without hesitation, I answered: "God."

Kathy smirked, knowing from experience what my answer would be. She and I have had many conversations about God, religion, death, and what comes after we die. I've always felt that since the beginning of time, God has continually allowed people to connect with their loved ones on the Other Side as one way of letting us mere mortals know that there's an afterlife and that God actually exists.

Kathy turned the conversation back to the Rosary book, and her co-worker interrupted again with a derogatory huff. "Praying the Rosary? What powers do you think those beads possess? Why pray to saints? And who is Mary? Why pray to her? Why not go directly to the Source?"

I smiled politely, out of respect to Kathy (who was now rolling her eyes), and responded in a way that made it clear to all present that I wasn't about to engage in a debate over this woman's religious beliefs. I never enter into debates or try to defend my belief in God or in communicating with the Other Side, because, to me, there's simply nothing to debate or defend. God and the Other Side are as real to me as the air I breathe.

But this woman did get me thinking about the other attacks that will inevitably come my way after this book is published. Most of them will likely come from the anonymous cowards on the Internet who type out their venom while safely hidden from view behind a computer screen. I'd like to say a prayer for all of them, hoping that they'll come to see beyond the walls they've built up around themselves. . . .

Through writing and discussing this book, I've learned that some people already have such a strong Prayer Dialogue with God that they know with certainty that they're connected, and they feel that they can just "dial up" their own personal "Hotline to Heaven" whenever they feel the need. But others don't feel *any* connection at all, or don't know where to begin, or feel abandoned or lost. Some wonder if God even exists.

What I've discovered is simple: Prayer is prayer, just as water is water, I don't care how you bottle it. I hope *Practical*

*Praying* helps you find the ability to connect to the Hotline to Heaven in your own life, and tap in to the abundance of the universe through the power and energy of prayer.

In this book, I'm going to share with you how I've been using the Rosary as my weapon of spiritual defense for more than 20 years. I've also included the official method of praying the Rosary as sanctioned by the Catholic Church. In addition, enclosed you will find a CD that will help you meditate and pray when you feel the need for further guidance. (I'd also like to extend a special thank you to actress Roma Downey for lending her "angelic" voice on the CD to assist you on your journey.)

Once again, why did I write this book? My goal is simple: to inspire you to start your own Prayer Dialogue so that you can strengthen your personal connection to the Other Side.

⊂⊙⊃

# Chapter Two

# *My Own Journey*

B eing raised Catholic, I was taught to use the Rosary as a tool in my religious education. But like other kids, I just went through the motions of counting the beads without really understanding what it all meant. Like the alphabet and the multiplication tables, I memorized the prayers and was able to recite them on cue. I moved through my religion classes and received the various standard sacraments given to all practicing Catholics—from baptism to marriage.

As a child, I remember thinking that the Rosary might have magical powers. During one of my classes, a nun told us that it was incredibly powerful in "stomping out Satan" and "destroying all evil." Those words may have been meant to instill a sense of heavenly protection in us, but quite frankly, they scared the hell out me! My pet name for that nun was Sister Mary Terror, and she made sure that all of us kids left the classroom that day armed with our plastic Rosaries so that we could ward off the evil of Satan on our own.

When I got home, I hung my pale-green plastic Rosary from the mirror of my bedroom bureau. Little did I know that it was a glow-in-the-dark version, and after sitting in the sunlight for hours, it was fully charged. When I rolled over in the middle of the night and saw all the beads lit up, I thought they were floating in the air. Then I remembered that they were designed to "stomp out Satan" and concluded that if they'd suddenly been activated, it could mean only one thing: Satan was in my bedroom!

My screams woke up everyone in the house, and quite possibly everyone on my block. My entire family took turns assuring me that Satan had better things to do than pay a late-night visit to our Long Island address to pick up my soul. It took a while, but I was eventually able to fall back to sleep. The next morning my family couldn't stop chuckling over Sister Mary Terror's thoughtful gift.

Like all Catholic kids, I knew about praying and was taught that I had nothing to fear as long as I embraced God. But I honestly never really stopped to process the meaning behind the teachings. I memorized the words without grasping their significance. It was just another thing a kid was told to do over and over, like "Eat your vegetables." I recited my prayers as fast as I could to get them over with. I'm sure it sounded something like this: "Ourfather whosewartsinheaven . . . howdybeandyename . . . thykingkongcome . . . dyedwoolbeworninhevin."

Now admit it, you're laughing right now because, as a kid, you probably did your own fair share of speed-praying. And who knows? You might have had a Sister Mary Terror and a glow-in-the-dark-stomping-out-Satan experience yourself.

At any rate, while I learned about the Rosary and praying as a boy, it took me a long time to figure out what they meant, and even longer to understand their wonderful power.

## My Personal Discovery: The Rosary Revisited

Sister Mary Terror may have given me my first Rosary, but she didn't introduce me to the crucifix and string of beads that would become so important to me later in life. That honor belongs solely to my grandmother. I watched her pray every morning and evening—a routine she kept up until the day she died. I thought it was part of her Grandma role—wear lots of perfume, cook for an army, and pray when you wake up and before bed—I sure didn't think it was something young people did. Then one evening around the Easter holidays when I couldn't sleep, I stayed up to watch two late-night movies that inspire me to this day. The first was *The Song of Bernadette,* about a teenage girl in 1858 France who has a vision of "the beautiful lady" the townspeople believe to be the Virgin Mary. The second was also about a "Marian apparition"—*The Miracle of Our Lady of Fatima,* a film based on the real-life events of three shepherd children to whom the Virgin Mary appeared in 1917 near the town of Fatima, Portugal.

I was so transfixed by the stories that I immediately asked my family if they were true, or just based on some Bible fables used to teach Christian lessons. My family was unanimous in their response: The stories were true. I'd come to learn that these films were both about the same woman, the mother of Jesus who was known by many names: the Virgin Mary, the Lady of Light, the Blessed Mother, Mother of God, and the Queen of Heaven, to name a just a few.

The stories made an indelible impression on me, but I didn't really dwell on them. I figured that these kinds of miraculous "visions" happened in the "olden days" in countries far, far away from my modern American home. As I got older, I realized that they happened everywhere in the world, and by the time I was a teenager, I'd found out that they even happened on Long Island.

When I was in high school, a lot of people talked about Veronica Lueken, a woman who claimed that she was receiving messages from the Virgin Mary, and that at this apparition site, *this* Mary wanted to be known as Our Lady of the Roses. I remembered first hearing about Veronica years earlier when my Aunt Rachel got hold of a film about her. At least 30 people from my extended family crammed into Aunt Rachel's basement in Queens to watch this pseudo-documentary about the woman who saw Mary. I guess I was too young to really get into the story, and I remember that the only profound thought I had that night was that I wanted my mom to stop at McDonald's on the way home. I'd like to say that I was inspired by the Virgin Mary appearing a short drive from my house, but at the time, the prospect of a Big Mac was far more enticing.

Years later, when I was just embarking on my psychic and spiritual awakening, "The Lady" returned, and this time I was a little more receptive. I was managing a local video store, and a customer randomly gave me a laminated rose petal embossed on a beige card. Written on it were the words: BLESSED BY OUR LADY OF THE ROSES, BAYSIDE.

*Bayside, Queens? Get out of here!* I thought. Of course I had to check it out, though. I mean, this wasn't only happening in the present day *and* in the United States, but it was happening in a public park not 20 minutes from my house.

For the next few months, I kept going back to this park. If I remember correctly, these "Lady of the Roses" gatherings were held on the 13th of every month. You never knew quite what to expect, and never knew that Mary had appeared to Veronica until she went into an "ecstasy," a sort of mystical frenzy. However, what I *do* remember very clearly about those warm, breezy summer evenings are the brilliantly painted skies above the throngs of people who'd traveled to Flushing Meadows Park to see this strange housewife and mother of five try to commune with the Holy Mother.

One evening in particular, I witnessed one of the most beautiful sunsets I've ever seen. It was truly amazing. As thousands of people united in prayer, the sky softened into a multicolored palette of beautiful blues, pinks, and greens swirling around the remnants of soft white clouds as they slowly faded from the dazzling horizon. Honestly, I felt as though I were in a Spielberg movie. To this day, if I ever see a sunset that resembles the one I was so struck by that night, I stop for a moment to say a few prayers and show my appreciation for what I'll always call an "Our Lady sky."

At the time, I was a young teen who was exploring my own beliefs and philosophies regarding spirituality and religion. Sometimes I took a friend with me; once I took my grandmother; but each and every time, my Aunt Roseanne came along. Ironically, my mother, who was extremely spiritual, chose never to attend—not even once. When I questioned her about it, her response was simple: "My faith is strong; besides, I don't believe that the Church has recognized *her,* the apparition site, or any of it at all."

My mother was right. The Church did not, and still has not, recognized Veronica or the supposed apparitions at the site in Bayside, Queens. But by that stage of my life, I was fascinated with anything deemed supernatural, and this fit the bill perfectly. I'd recently had a life-altering experience with a psychic who'd given me an astounding, dead-on reading, predicting that I'd go on to become a well-known medium. I was determined to explore anything to do with this new world of energy and psychic phenomena.

Having personally attended Veronica's events several times, I'm sure you want to know if I think she was *really* speaking to the Virgin Mary. I'm sorry to report that I have no idea. But by just being there, I experienced a spiritual awakening—I believe that if Mary *was* there, she was communicating with all of us, not just Veronica.

I came away from these events feeling a newfound peacefulness. Whether or not Veronica, who died in 1995, was in communication with Mary no longer mattered to me—these events showed me how to begin my own Prayer Dialogue with God. I'd seen this woman unite people in prayer, and I'd seen the Rosary prayed for hours on end. It was a turning point for me in understanding the universality of prayer, and I began connecting to my own Hotline to Heaven in my everyday life. Since that summer, I've always carried the Rosary with me. It's either in my pocket, car, wallet, or sometimes all the above. Often, I find myself giving away my Rosaries to others who I think need them more than I do.

## Prayer and Illness: A Medical Miracle?

My interest in prayer and the Rosary continued in a very profound way. In 1989, my mother was diagnosed with a rare form of lung cancer, and her prognosis was terminal. At that point, after spending nearly five years studying spirituality and metaphysics and embracing the Rosary, my faith was extremely strong, and I "knew" that there was an afterlife. My belief in God was unwavering

So when my mom was diagnosed, I prayed the Rosary for a health miracle. I prayed, begged, even *demanded* that she be cured. I read about miraculous healings and tumors that spontaneously disappeared, or illnesses that inexplicably went into remission. I wanted her to be one of them, a modern-day medical miracle. I was determined to see her cured by my power of continual positive praying.

I had no idea at the time that I'd already "been shown" the outcome of my mother's illness.

For years, at my seminars and on *Crossing Over,* I've talked about my experiences with my mother's passing. But this is something I haven't shared until now. You see, about a year before my mother was diagnosed, I had what I thought at the time was just a strange dream. In it, I walked into the bathroom near my bedroom and saw my grandmother's statue of the Infant of Prague sitting on the counter. In reality, this statue belonged on my grandmother's dresser in her bedroom downstairs, with the myriad other saints on her pseudo-altar. It would never be upstairs, because my grandmother would have too much difficulty climbing the stairs to see it.

Now, the only thing I knew about this statue at that time was that it was some type of representation of baby Jesus with a crown and a red cloak, that Italians put a dime under it, and that it had to be facing a door.

Anyway, I'm dreaming this . . . yet I'm desperately trying to be rational and analyze what's going on. I'm wondering, *Why is the statue here? Maybe my little cousin moved it while he was playing. I better put it back before my grandmother realizes it's gone and flips out!* This is when the dream gets really freaky. When I reach out to pick up the statue, it turns into an animated Claymation figure and begins to move and talk! Well, even in my dream, my good Catholic upbringing kicked in, and I dropped to my knees and bowed my head. And then I was told three things:

1. There was going to be a role reversal in my family: I was going to have to be the strong one and take care of my mother, because she was going to need my help.

2. "Remember pancoast! Remember it by thinking, *Pan American flies the coast!*"

3. To this day I still can't remember what the third thing was. I've even been hypnotized to try to recall it. (But for those of you reading this, please don't write to tell me what you think it is. I feel that in time, if I'm supposed to know, it will be revealed to me.)

I woke up and thought, *What an odd dream!* But that's all it was—a dream, nothing more. I got out of bed and went downstairs to see whether the statue was on my grandmother's dresser. Sure enough, there it was—right where it was supposed to be. Like an idiot, I was standing there staring at it, half expecting it to turn into a Claymation figure and break out into a tap-dancing number (it didn't), when my Aunt Roseanne walked into the room and asked me what I was doing. I told her about the dream, remembering every detail, as though I'd memorized it for a test.

A year later, I was preparing to go on a long-planned trip to Venezuela with my cousin and a friend when, after a series of misdiagnoses, doctors discovered the tumor on my mother's lung. At first, they weren't forthcoming about either the type of tumor she had or her prognosis. Eventually, all the medical personnel who examined her agreed that the tumor was malignant—but I believed that it was benign.

When my mother was being admitted into the second-to-last hospital she was to stay in, my Aunt Roseanne and I were sitting in the admitting office. As the registrar wheeled my mom down the hall and my dad followed, I asked my aunt to watch the door. At that time, I was in my second year of college earning a degree in hospital administration and had already learned a thing or two about the business side of health care. I knew that when you were admitted to a hospital, they had to write down an "admitting diagnosis." So, with my aunt keeping watch, I opened my mother's file on the desk and read the diagnosis. It said:

### Admitting Diagnosis = Pancoast Tumor

*Pancoast?* I closed the file and looked at my aunt with a quizzical expression. I whispered the name of the tumor, and she made a face like a dog hearing a high-pitched noise. *Huh?*

I knew I'd heard that word before, and so did she. As we drove home together, we struggled to figure out where we'd heard it: Was it a TV character? The name of a book? Maybe a movie we'd both seen? We were stumped. I didn't put it together with the dream that I'd had—and had told her about—a year earlier. At least, not until I spoke to my friend Shelley.

My mom's surgery was scheduled for May 25, two days before I was supposed to leave for my trip to Venezuela. I remembered thinking, *Some psychic I am—I schedule a trip at the most inopportune time possible.* I wanted to cancel, but everyone around me insisted that I go, clear my head, and come back refreshed. My father even threatened that he wouldn't let me visit my mother during the week I was supposed to be away because he knew that if she found out I hadn't gone, she'd realize there was something severely wrong.

My rock at that time was my good friend and fellow psychic Shelley Peck. She called me every day just to make sure that I was "talking." I remember her calling me and asking me what airline I was flying to Venezuela. I responded that it was AVENSA. Her response was haunting: "Oh . . . I don't know why, but I thought you were flying Pan Am. You know, Pan American flies the coast!"

*Bam!* It all came flooding back to me in a rush: The dream, the message about the role reversal and that I'd be needed by my mother, and most important, *Pancoast.* Shelley was an amazing psychic, and I immediately asked her why she'd said what she did.

"Obviously you needed to hear it," she replied.

---

That afternoon I found myself sitting in the medical-reference section of the public library researching Pancoast tumors. I learned a lot—namely, that my mother had six months to live. I immediately began to pray.

I'd remembered that hundreds of people received miraculous cures and intercessions regarding their health when they went to apparition sites and bathed in the water where "The Lady of Light" had appeared. I thought that maybe, just maybe, a modern-day miracle would happen . . . right here on Long Island.

Like anyone going through a difficult time, whose world is about to change forever, I was reaching out for Divine assistance. I prayed like crazy that all the stories of miracles I'd heard and read about over the years would come true for my mother. I'm a big fan of getting validation, so I asked for a sign that my prayers would be answered.

During a meditation, I was "shown" an image of a statue of the Blessed Mother, and I had a strong feeling as to what this meant: I was supposed to erect a statue of her in the back room of my grandmother's home. It was to be an outdoor statue, but I had to display it indoors, surrounded by plants, so everyone could see it. (Yes, I was shown this much detail during my meditation.) My spirit guides also told me that I'd be given a sign that would validate all this at a later date. The Boys told me that the sign would be a bigger statue of the Blessed Mother surrounded by green bushes, with an even larger statue in the distance behind it on a hill.

I immediately went to the local garden-supply store, found a statue of the Virgin Mary, and brought it home. I told my aunt and grandmother that it had to be put in the back room and not touched by anyone. They looked at me like I'd lost my mind. I'm sure they were thinking, *Leave the boy alone . . . poor kid, he's just 19 years old, and he's trying to find a way to deal with all this.*

The next week I was scheduled to do a lecture in the Hamptons at the far end of Long Island. As I was driving out there, I noticed a road sign that said: OUR LADY OF THE ISLAND. Of course I had to check it out. My validation came to me as soon as I pulled up to this Catholic shrine in Eastport, Long Island. Not only did I find an outside statue of the Blessed Mother in the bushes there, but I also saw a huge statue dedicated to her off in the distance behind her, on a hilltop. It was a beautiful and peaceful discovery, and it seemed in every way to be the answer to my prayers. I was sure it was the validation I was waiting for that my mother would be cured. To me, it was a clear sign that a modern-day miracle was about to occur.

In the weeks leading up to my mom's actual passing—more than a year and a half after my dream about the Infant of Prague—I had another dream. In this one, I was downstairs in my grandmother's living room watching television. Suddenly I noticed a small six-inch statue of the Blessed Mother on a shelf above the TV. The statue became animated and started to move just like the Infant of Prague had done in the earlier dream. Once again, the moving statue unnerved me, and I got on my knees and bowed my head. As I prayed, my Aunt Rachel walked into the house, looked at me praying, smiled a teary-eyed smile, and then ran upstairs where my mother lay dying. Then I heard the message:

*"Some people can't handle certain situations and react differently from the way you might want them to. Be understanding. Be unconditional. Be forgiving."*

The words reminded me of a recent, minor misunderstanding I'd had with my Aunt Rachel, after which I'd snapped at her angrily.

When I woke up the next morning, I immediately ran into my mom's bedroom to make sure she was still alive. I told her about the dream, hoping to get a response from her like, "Wow . . . that's so weird!" But before she had a chance to say anything, my Aunt Rachel walked into the bedroom. What she said next totally freaked out my mother and me:

"Prin [my mom's name], I had the most beautiful dream last night. I dreamt that I walked into Momma's house, and in the living room was a little boy with platinum blonde hair, who reminded me of Johnny when he was a baby, and he was kneeling in front of a huge six-foot statue of Our Lady and laying yellow roses at her feet. I think she's working on your behalf, and that all our prayers are being heard."

My mom and I looked at each other like, *Do you want to tell her? I don't!* We kept my dream to ourselves, but were completely intrigued by the whole thing. My aunt and I made up, putting our minor bickering behind us, and my mom and I decided to just wait and see how this story was going to play out. I believed that, because of our family's love for each other, our strong faith, and our heartfelt prayers, my mother would soon be healed. But the next time she went into the hospital, the doctors told us something different—that her cancer was progressing and that she would not, and should not, come home. In fact, to deter us from bringing her home, they told us in painful and graphic detail that my mother was going to die—and that it was going to be a very messy death.

"Our girl is coming home," one of my aunts briskly informed the doctors, "and if she *is* dying, she'll do so with the love of family around her . . . not strangers."

On October 5, 1989, at approximately 4 A.M., my mother drew her last breath. Her passing was peaceful and calm—exactly the *opposite* of the nightmarish death the doctors had predicted. Quite honestly, she left this world with a smile on her face, and a single tear rolling down her left cheek.

Some people feel relief when a very ill loved one crosses over because it means that they're out of pain and "in a good place." Me? I felt betrayed, angry, and spiritually bankrupt. Why didn't my spirit guides tell me earlier about my mom's cancer so that we could have caught it sooner and not wasted time with doctors and their misdiagnoses? What about all the prayers I'd said, and the "validation" statues I'd encountered? What about the dreams? Was it all in my imagination—had I wanted to believe so desperately in my faith and prayers that I conjured up the shrine I found while driving to the Hamptons?

My world became a dark and gloomy place. Then one day, weeks later, I was pulling a thick pile of letters and flyers from our crammed mailbox when I dropped it all onto the ground.

Now I've heard that signs come in unique ways, but in the *mail?*

There at my feet was a newsletter addressed to me from the Association of the Miraculous Medal, another level of devotion to the Rosary and the Virgin Mary. The pamphlet had landed on the ground and opened to a specific story—it was about a woman who was dying of lung cancer, and had been written by her 19-year-old son. I picked it up and stood there, frozen to the spot, reading about this teenage boy who was the same age as me, and who'd prayed for a cure for his mother who, like my mom, had gotten a terminal diagnosis.

The parallels between our two stories stunned me. This young man described how the doctors had predicted a gloomy, painful death for his mother, but instead, she'd died with a smile on her face. Everything he and his mother had gone through was identical to what had happened with my family— I could have written this article myself.

While I stood there shivering in a pile of unopened mail, I suddenly realized that the miracle I'd prayed so hard for had actually occurred. No, my mother's cancer wasn't cured— but what I kept praying for was Divine assistance, and that's exactly what I believe my mom and I received. Her passing defied the doctors' dire predictions—that her body would break down in a cruel and ugly way. Even the hospice-care providers were awestruck by how "clean" and peaceful her passing had been.

"God gave you all a beautiful gift in her passing," said Claire, her hospice nurse.

I truly believe to this day that my mother's peaceful transition came about as a direct result of my family and me praying with such "intention" during her illness.

Would I have preferred a Divine healing? Of course! But I've learned that we're all on our own path, and we each come into this life to learn and teach specific lessons. I believe that my mom's passing was a final class in which she was both student and teacher. I've said repeatedly that if my mother didn't pass when she did, I wouldn't have devoted my energy and life's work to learning and teaching about the Other Side. It was her passing that created the need for me to study more about the afterlife. Her passing is still teaching me, and this book is just one example of how her spirit, love, and wisdom endures.

I took away a valuable lesson from my mother's death. I learned that while you may not receive exactly what you *think* you're praying for, your prayers will likely bring you what you need . . . as well as what God intends for you as part of the "bigger plan." This experience solidified my belief in the power of prayer and the Rosary, and how they can help us through life, illness, and death.

*The power of prayer can intercede in our lives*
*and assist us on our journeys in ways that*
*our minds can't always comprehend.*

(By the way, not long after I received the pamphlet in the mail, my skeptical side kicked in and I decided to find out why it was sent to me. It turns out that I'd never subscribed to that newsletter and had never even made a donation to any charities affiliated with the association that publishes it, and yet . . . the pamphlet had my name on its impeccably typed label. I never did receive that newsletter again.)

# Our Lady of Guadalupe

As I've mentioned, I've had an ongoing affinity with the Rosary and "Our Lady," as my grandmother called the Virgin Mary, ever since my early teens. She's actually become a symbol for me in my work—unfortunately, it's not such a good symbol for people on *this* side when I get an image of Mary. For those of you familiar with what I do, you know that I get specific images from my spirit guides to help me relay messages from the Other Side. For instance, when I see boxes, it means that someone's moving; a fluttering in my stomach means someone's pregnant; and a green light symbolizes that someone still living can move on with their life with the blessings of their loved ones on the Other Side. But when I see the Virgin Mary, look out! It's a sure sign that someone I know is going to cross over.

I don't want people to take this the wrong way—when I say "see" the Holy Mother, I'm not saying that I'm a "visionary," that I see apparitions, or that I'm channeling Mary or any other saint. Got it? I want to make that clear right from the start, because I can just imagine the line of questioning I'm going to get on my next talk-show appearance: "So tell me, Mr. Edward . . . when does the Virgin Mary come to you, and how long have you two been having these little chats?"

As I've said, when I see an image of Mary, it's just a symbol the Boys use so that I know someone connected to me is going to cross over—and I have plenty of painful examples to illustrate this. I've already written at length about how I kept seeing images of the Blessed Virgin before my mother died. But I also received images of Mary shortly before my Aunt Rachel was diagnosed with cancer in 1996, and again when my grandmother Josephine, Rachel's mother, became deathly ill later that same year.

At the time, I was still doing readings for clients in my home office. I remember this one session with a mother and a daughter when, in the middle of the reading, I began to notice what looked like a spot of light the size of a dime beginning to form over the mother's shoulder. The small circle began to grow larger and larger and take on different shades of color . . . blues, reds, oranges, and golds. I'd never experienced anything like this before, and I remember thinking, *Okaaaaay, this is new . . . I'll just go with it.*

Soon the lights and colors began to fuse into an image that appeared to me as a painting of the Virgin Mary—but not the kind I was used to seeing in churches or books. This one was of a dark-skinned woman with dark hair. She was radiant, with a serene beauty. In my mind, I heard a soft, but crystal clear, whisper: *"Guadalupe."*

And let me tell you, as a medium, there are times when I have trouble getting simple names like "Bill," "Bob," or even my own, "John." Usually the names I hear come to me either too quickly or too muffled for me to make out much more than the first initials.

Not that night. *Guadalupe.* Clear as a bell.

I asked the mother and daughter if they had any special devotion to the Blessed Mother, and if so, was there something called Our Lady of Guadalupe that she was connected to? They shook their heads, "Uh, nope." I told them exactly what I was seeing and asked them if they were Catholic and if the image meant anything at all to them.

They *were* Catholic, but neither had a clue what this message could possibly mean to them, and I was at a complete loss. It was frustrating to have an image and name come though with such clarity and not be able to connect the message with a meaning. What was I missing?

I asked the clients if it would be all right for me to interrupt their session to make a call to my Aunt Anna—a very religious woman—in the hopes that she could provide some insight on the name and image I was getting. When I got her on the phone and asked if she'd ever heard of Our Lady of Guadalupe, she uttered a resounding, "Oh yeah!"

I asked her in what country the apparition site existed, and she responded in the vaguest fashion imaginable. "Oh . . . you know . . . in one of those countries out there."

I felt like laughing out loud, but knew that my clients wouldn't appreciate my guffawing in the middle of their session.

I hung up and continued with the reading, and other details started coming through: There was an image of a beautiful wall mosaic of Our Lady of Guadalupe—I could see two people standing in front of the mosaic, and a bouquet of yellow roses carefully arranged on the floor beside the wall.

The images got nothing but blank stares and confused looks from my clients. It was disappointing, but like other readings where clients don't understand something at the time, I figured that they'd eventually make the connection and end up sending me a letter validating all the details.

After they left, I sat down at my desk and started doing some paperwork, when something caught my eye. I looked up, startled. There she was again, as bright as can be imagined, the same colorful image of the dark-skinned, vibrant lady with a gold light shimmering all around her. I immediately sat back in my chair and thought, *Uh-oh . . . this definitely means something for me . . . but what?*

It was a very unsettling feeling, so I called my friend Father Patrick to ask him about this image and if he knew what it meant.

"You called the right person," he told me. "I was ordained as a priest on December 12th—the feast day of Our Lady of Guadalupe."

He suggested that I visit St. Hugh's Church, which isn't too far from my home and has a beautiful chapel devoted to Our

Lady of Guadalupe. "And the church has a beautiful mosaic tile image of her on the wall," he added.

I nearly dropped the phone. It was the exact image I'd just received during the mother/daughter reading.

"Perhaps Our Lady is trying to share something with you," Father Patrick suggested. "I think you should just go with it."

Go with it? I didn't want to. The first time I "went with" one of these things it resulted in the death of my mother. I didn't want to see anyone else in my family getting sick, so I figured I'd just take a pass on visiting the mosaic. But I couldn't stop the references to Our Lady of Guadalupe from coming through fast and furious. I'll give you just a few examples of the images I received within a two-week period:

- Psychic Lydia Clar, the woman who did my first reading, called to ask if I had any affiliation with the Shrine of Our Lady of Guadalupe. During a meditation, she'd had a mental image of me making a pilgrimage to it.

- I received a brochure from a tour group promoting a pilgrimage to Mexico City and the Shrine of Our Lady of Guadalupe.

- Lydia called again to say that she'd
  "seen" me being pulled toward the shrine
  and that I would see the faces of many
  children all around Our Lady's image.

- While running errands, I came across a new
  Catholic supply store with a poster of Our
  Lady of Guadalupe figured prominently in its
  window. It was surrounded by dozens of photos
  of children—just as Lydia had predicted.

- When I walked into the store, a saleslady
  immediately approached and, without any
  prompting, handed me a statue of Our Lady.
  "I thought you asked me for this. Was it you?"
  No, it wasn't, but I bought two of them right away.

- At a family gathering, a friend turned to me
  and asked me if I liked the new charm on
  her necklace . . . Our Lady of Guadalupe.

- A gift that Shelley Peck had given me
  years earlier—a metallic frame with the
  face inlaid of . . . you got it—fell onto
  the floor for no apparent reason.

- It suddenly dawned on me that a gift I'd bought for my mother seven years earlier while vacationing in Venezuela was actually a funky, blown-glass statue of the Blessed Mother . . . and yup, it was Our Lady of Guadalupe once again.

- I then noticed for the first time that the plaque over my grandmother Josephine's bed, which had been there for years and years, was an image of Our Lady of Guadalupe.

All this—and much more I haven't mentioned—happened in such a short period of time that it became unnerving. Consequently, I began reading up on the history of this saint. What really stood out to me was the fact that she was continually referred to as "The Mother of all Mothers." She was called this because she's depicted wearing a garment worn by native Mexican women when they're pregnant.

In the following months, more and more references to Our Lady of Guadalupe kept coming my way, and pretty soon everyone in my family was getting them as well. We were all waiting to see where this was leading. It was during this barrage of signs that my cousin Assunta decided to meet me at the Chapel of Our Lady of Guadalupe. She arrived carrying an armful of yellow roses, and immediately, the images from the reading weeks earlier flashed through my mind:

*Two people . . . mosaic tile wall . . . yellow roses . . .*

I was unnerved yet again. The messages of that mother/daughter session were unfolding in front of me. Assunta and I walked into the empty chapel and were impressed by the wall—it was as beautiful as Father Patrick had said. As we sat in silence and prayed, we both noticed something odd—the way the light was hitting the tiles made it appear as though Our Lady of Guadalupe had begun to cry. Once again my skeptical side kicked in, and I had to get up and touch her lovely face. Thankfully, it was dry.

Suddenly, Assunta looked at me and smiled. "I know why we're here," she said. "It's about your mom."

Her words jolted me, and I suddenly understood the real reason we were there. It wasn't about *my* mother, it was about *hers,* my Aunt Rachel. I knew then with certainty that she wouldn't beat the cancer she'd been diagnosed with.

A few months later, as both my Aunt Rachel and my grandmother were preparing to pass—they actually died 12 days apart—I understood the meaning of the Our Lady of Guadalupe message. It represented the passing of the mother and the child, the passing of an older and younger person.

The message was further validated at my grandmother's bedside when her nurse walked in and said, "Josephine, you have a beautiful family and a lot of love around you. You are the mother of all mothers!"

My Aunt Roseanne was standing on the opposite side of my grandmother's bed and had to look away as tears filled her eyes. She knew all too well what that message I'd received so many weeks earlier had meant. My grandmother passed on September 5, 1996, and my Aunt Rachel crossed over on the 17th of the same month. Both women had one of the statues I'd bought of Our Lady of Guadalupe on their bedside tables when they died.

One month later I got another sign.

My wife, Sandra, and I were in Miami at a ballroom-dancing convention. She had to get up early the next morning to compete, but I didn't—I just felt like watching TV and vegging out. While she was sleeping, I sat on the floor munching on chocolate-chip cookies when I saw a brilliant flash of light by the doorway of our room.

"Oh my God, it's happening again!" I exclaimed.

Sandra bolted upright in bed and stared at my panic-stricken face. It's not easy being married to a psychic, and for Sandra it can sometimes be downright annoying. Anyway, I told her what I was seeing—an image of Our Lady of Fatima in Portugal. I recognized it immediately because it was one of the first apparition sites I'd ever heard about.

Sandra began to cry. "It's my grandmother, John," she managed. "She's next . . . she's *in* Portugal."

The phone rang early the next morning. By that afternoon, Sandra was on a plane to Portugal for her grandmother's funeral.

## Pilgrimage

Even though the symbol of Mother Mary, in all her many variations, has often meant the death of one of my family members, I have a great devotion to, and faith in, her. So much so that I've made two pilgrimages to the shrine of Our Lady of Guadalupe in Mexico City to strengthen my "Prayer Dialogue" connection with her, pay my respects, and show my gratitude.

My first trip was in 1998, after the publication of my first book, *One Last Time*. I'd promised myself that I'd make the pilgrimage if the book hit the *New York Times* bestseller list as a thank-you to the Holy Mother.

But getting to the bestseller list was going to mean doing a book tour and lots of media publicity, and the tour couldn't have gotten off to a worse start. First of all, I had an absolutely terrible experience while being interviewed by a well-known and widely syndicated radio host. All I'll say about it is that it was a vile interview, and while I held my own, it poisoned the whole process of promoting a book that I deeply cared about. When I finished the interview, I thought, *Who needs this kind of abuse? To hell with the bestseller list!*

I pulled my Rosary out of my pocket and prayed that the rest of my tour would go off without a hitch. I was concerned that bad interviews would damage my reputation and hurt the many people who trusted me and who'd been helped by the thousands of readings I'd done throughout my career. And I also wanted my book to be well received so that I could get my message to as many people as possible. So I said my prayers with the Rosary and went to bed, hoping that the rest of the 12-city promotional tour would be better.

I guess this is another good example of how I use practical praying in everyday life, and how it can help us all in times of pain or crisis. After my prayers, the rest of my media tour went great! So as soon as I got home, I booked the trip to Mexico.

When I got there, the car service I'd arranged to pick me up at the airport in Mexico City was a no-show, and I walked outside into the confusion and chaos of one of the world's most densely populated cities—boisterous crowds, thick plumes of exhaust, and endless lines of people waiting for whatever they were waiting for. My spirit guides flashed a warning image to me that I was about to be pickpocketed, and I pulled my wallet from my back pocket and tucked it into one in front. About a minute later, in the crush of the crowd, I felt someone's hand make a quick dig into my back pocket. I immediately prayed for help—and thanked the Boys for the heads-up.

I finally got to my hotel room: tired, hungry, and a little worse for wear, but in one piece. I tried to order room service with my high school Spanish, but to my dismay found there was no *spaghetti con albondigas* (with meatballs) on the menu, so I got dressed and ventured back out into the city. My hotel was in an area called Zona Rosa—the Pink Zone—which I later learned was not a particularly safe section of the city. But at the time I wasn't feeling any sense of danger, just hunger. I prayed again that I'd find food. (Don't laugh! I told you I pray practically!)

My prayers were answered in two beautiful ways: I saw in the distance the familiar sight of a well-known American "shrine," the golden arches—a McDonald's! I had a very "happy meal," and on my way back to the hotel experienced another instance of Divine intervention: a Häagen-Dazs ice-cream parlor! This is what I survived on for three days in Mexico City. I know, I know . . . tough pilgrimage!

The next morning, December 12, 1998—the Feast Day of Our Lady of Guadalupe's first apparition to the young peasant boy Juan Diego—I attempted to visit the shrine. On the streets, I encountered complete madness. I'd hoped to take a taxi up to the Basilica where the shrine is, walk in, say my thank-you prayers to Our Lady and, having completed my mission, head home. But the concierge at the front desk attempted to explain to me in "Spanglish" that, on the Feast Day, it would be next to impossible to get a taxi to take me to the Basilica. They handed me a map and told me to walk. *Walk?* I'd just finished a 12-city book tour, and she expected me to walk through a strange city? I looked pleadingly at the concierge, but she was unsympathetic.

And so I began my journey toward the Basilica on foot, feeling dejected and a bit humbled. I was well on my way when a black sedan pulled up alongside me, and the window rolled down. In very poor English, the driver asked me if I wanted a ride to the Basilica. Although I never would have done so in New York City, I hopped in without hesitation or even asking him how he'd guessed where I was going. As we drove, the driver began chatting with me in his broken English, giving me a quick lesson in local history. He told me that years ago, someone tried to blow up the "cactus-cloth tilma" of Juan Diego—the clothing the young man was wearing when Our Lady appeared to him and that still showed Mary's image. He told me that everything was destroyed in the blast, except for Mary's image on the fabric.

When he dropped me off, I was four blocks and a small hill away from coming face-to-face with the image I'd first seen two years earlier during that incredible mother/daughter session in my home office.

When Our Lady of Guadalupe appeared to Juan Diego in the 1500s, she asked him to go to the bishop and convince him to build a church at the site. Juan did as she asked, but the bishop told Juan that he needed proof that he'd seen Our Lady. When Juan next saw her, she instructed him to pick flowers from the hill and return with them to the bishop. Juan reluctantly set out to do so, not expecting to find any because it was winter.

To his surprise, Juan found all kinds of beautiful flowers of many different colors, picked as many as he could carry in his cactus-cloth garment (known as a *tilma*), and headed back to see the bishop. Juan offered up the out-of-season blooms as proof of Our Lady's existence. When he placed the flowers at the bishop's feet, all the clergy in the room gasped and began to pray. You see, the image of Our Lady that Juan Diego had claimed to have seen and talked to was clearly imprinted on his cactus-cloth garment. This garment has been on display in the church and Basilica ever since. Scientists say it should have deteriorated centuries ago, but to this day, some 470 years later, it shows no sign of decay. To my limited knowledge, it's the only apparition site where an image has been left.

An incredible list of miracles, cures, and interventions are attributed to Our Lady of Guadalupe. Each year more than ten million people make the pilgrimage to her Basilica, making Mexico City home to the most popular Marian shrine in the world—and the most visited Catholic Church anywhere except the Vatican.

As I walked toward the Basilica, I became increasingly, and more profoundly, humbled. I saw people from all over the world there that day paying tribute to Our Lady. There were men and women of all ages and from all walks of life kneeling on the ground, their knees skinned and bleeding from hours of prolonged worship—all in the name of prayer. This is forever burned in my memory. I bore witness to a level of devotion and faith that would nourish any soul, Catholic or not. I've had a similar feeling when I've seen images of thousands of Muslims making the annual hajj, or pilgrimage, to Mecca.

I sat in the Basilica, just a few feet from the holy image, and prayed in thanks as I'd promised. The spiritual energy in the room was so overwhelming that I could only stay a few minutes before I began to feel completely drained. I made my way back to the spot where my driver had dropped me off, and there he was, waiting for me with a bottle of refreshingly cold water. I slumped in the backseat, exhausted, and looked forward to returning to my hotel for a hot shower and leisurely stroll to the Häagen-Dazs store for a post-shrine dessert. At least that was my plan . . . but my driver had another agenda.

Instead of heading back to the Zona Rosa district, I noticed that we were going away from my hotel, heading north and out of the city. The driver was trying to find out what I did for a living—as I struggled to come up with the word *psychic* or *medium* in Spanish, I was also trying to figure out where we were going. His English was limited, and my seven years of Spanish in school hadn't taught me enough to describe my admittedly unusual occupation.

"Yo soy un hombre quien habla con gente de mundos differente," I said to him, thinking it would roughly translate into: "I am a man who talks with people from different worlds." Okay, it wasn't exact, but I figured he'd catch the drift.

He stared at me in the rearview mirror as though I *was* from a different world. I tried a few more lame attempts and then tried to ask him, "Como se dice en español . . . uh . . . 'medium'?"

His eyes lit up, and he seemed to finally understand words I'd butchered with my meat-cleaver Spanish. "Ah, sí! Medium!" he said. I guess some things are universal!

Before I had a chance to ask him just exactly where we were going, he began to tell me that he, too, "had a bit of what I had," and I must trust that he was taking me to a very special place.

*Trust you?* I thought, nervously. *I'm in a foreign country heading God knows where with a complete stranger. Uh . . . okay . . . this must be the part of the program where the American heads off into the sunset and is never heard from again.*

But as it turned out, this guy actually had *a lot* of psychic ability and knew better than I as to what I needed at that moment in time.

He drove us about 30 miles north to the ancient city of Teotihuacán—a Nahuatl name meaning "the city of the Gods."

My new friend told me that he felt I had a "regalo" (gift) to both teach and help people spiritually. Just then, we passed a street called "Calle de los Muertos," or the "street of the dead." Imagine that!

Then he pointed out the two towering pyramids I'd somehow failed to notice until then—the Pyramid of the Sun and the Pyramid of the Moon—both more than 2,000 years old. He drove me to the bottom of the Pyramid of the Sun, which, as it turns out, is the third largest pyramid in the world.

"The rest of this journey you must do alone," he said, motioning for me to get out of the car and start walking. "Your soul is tired and drained and needs to be rejuvenated. That's why I brought you here."

It was weird, but by this point, our communication had become very clear. I don't remember if my Spanish had come back to me or if his English had suddenly improved. It didn't matter. Either way, we'd formed a bond and seemed to understand each other completely.

But as mystical as all this sounds, please know that through it all, I kept saying to myself, *You have got to be kidding me! Is this for real?*

I looked over at my new amigo, who'd begun instructing me on what to do when I reached the top of the pyramid. "You must hold up your palms toward the sun and stay in that position for as long as you feel the need," he said, pointing skyward.

I looked up at the pyramid and began to climb. I don't know how weary my *soul* was at the bottom of it, but let me tell you, after climbing 215 feet straight up, my *legs* were pretty darn weary when I got to the top. But I did get there, and as I stood on the flat plateau of stone I was overcome by a wave of emotion. There were more than 30 people doing exactly what my driver friend had told me to do—standing with arms outstretched and palms turned up toward the sun.

From my perch high above the earth, I felt rather small, like a grain of sand on a beach; but at the same time, I had a sense of being integrally connected with the entire universe. I felt at peace—and I was very, very thankful for everything in my life.

I stayed for more than an hour, praying the Rosary on my fingers. I prayed that I'd remain a clear and open channel for whatever teachings were intended to come through me. Then I said a little prayer of appreciation for the encouraging tour guide who had brought me to this wonderful place.

When I'd descended to the bottom of the pyramid, my amigo was there, waiting for me once again with a cold bottle of water. He asked me if I wanted to climb to the top of the Moon Pyramid next. I looked at him and let out a long sigh that said "No way!"

He laughed and told me that my soul must be nourished enough, but that my stomach must be empty. He tried to take me to a street-side grill, but I insisted on treating him to an all-American lunch at a fine dinning establishment he'd never been to before . . . you got it, we went to McDonald's.

After spending hours with this guy, I realized that I didn't even know his name. He smiled at me and introduced himself. He told me his name was *Jesus*.

I laughed until I couldn't breathe. The universe has a great sense of humor: I go on a spiritual sojourn and wind up having a Happy Meal with Jesus!

꒰ ꒱

# Chapter Three

# *Using the Rosary*

U sing the Rosary is a great way to focus your thoughts and energies— whether you're using the official Church method or the practical-praying method. It can help you become more centered and open, therefore allowing you to "pray with intention." By this, I mean praying with a specific thought or wish in mind. When you do so, you're helping yourself believe, create, and achieve in whatever areas of your life you desire.

In a way, it's like positive thinking: If you focus on a goal and visualize it, you're instructing your mind to believe in and achieve that goal. If you pray with "intention" and concentrate on your prayers, you're again creating a "better" phone line to the spirit world and clarifying what you're praying for.

But prayers not only need to be specific, they need to be heartfelt. If you rattle through the Rosary, mouthing the prayers mindlessly as if you're reciting the alphabet, you'll be completely disconnected from the energy of the experience. I believe that you have to be *in* the moment. I don't think it matters if that moment is 30 seconds or 30 minutes—just be a part of it, not *apart* from it.

If you're driving, don't you need to keep your eyes open and on the road? What happens if you don't focus all your attention on that task? Clearly, the outcome would be disastrous. Of course I'm not implying that if you don't pray, your life will crash and burn against the guardrail, but I do believe that when you really focus your prayer energy and listen carefully for God's voice, your learning accelerates to 90 miles per hour and you can be in complete control of both your direction and your destination. Unfortunately, I think that many people who don't embrace a concept of God or of praying end up walking to their life's destination.

In this chapter, I'm going to give you the "official" way to pray the Rosary, and then in the next chapter, I'll show you the practical-praying way. Please know that neither is better than the other—just make sure that you're focused and praying with intention.

## Crown of Roses

The word *Rosary* translates to "Crown of Roses." Our Lady has revealed to several people that each time they say a *Hail Mary,* they're giving her a beautiful rose, and that each complete Rosary makes her a crown of roses. Since the rose is the queen of flowers, so the Rosary is the queen of all devotions.

The Rosary is made up of two aspects: *mental prayer* and *vocal prayer.* Mental prayer consists of silently saying the prayers associated with the beads in the Rosary, and contemplating the various aspects of the life of Jesus and his mother, Mary, also known as the Virgin Mary, the Blessed Mother, or Our Lady. The *decades* (divisions of the Rosary consisting of five sets of ten beads) are also referred to as "Mysteries," and were originally divided into the Five Joyful Mysteries, the Five Sorrowful Mysteries, and the Five Glorious Mysteries. In 2002, Pope John Paul II added the Five Luminous Mysteries (or Mysteries of Light).

Vocal prayer consists of saying aloud 15 (or sometimes 5) decades of the *Hail Mary*, each decade headed by an Our Father, while at the same time meditating on and contemplating the 15 principal virtues that Jesus and Mary practiced in the 15 Mysteries of the Holy Rosary. The complete Rosary consists of 15 decades, but is more commonly said in 5.

So, the Rosary is a blessed blending of mental and vocal prayer in which we honor and learn to imitate the Mysteries and the Virtues of the life, death, passion, and glory of Jesus and Mary. It's said that the origin of the Rosary dates back to 1214 in a miraculous way, when Our Lady appeared to St. Dominic and gave it to him as a powerful means of converting the heretics and other nonbelievers or sinners of the time period. Since then, the devotion has spread around the world with incredible and miraculous results.

## Prayers of the Rosary

*The Sign of the Cross:* In the name of the Father, the Son, and of the Holy Spirit. Amen.

*Apostles' Creed:* I believe in God the Father Almighty, Creator of Heaven and Earth, and in Jesus Christ, his only son, our lord; who was conceived by the power of the Holy Spirit, born of the Virgin Mary, suffered under Pontius Pilate, was crucified, died, and was buried. He descended to the dead; on the third day he rose again. He ascended into Heaven and sits at the right hand of the Father. He will come again to judge the living and the dead. I believe in the Holy Spirit, the Holy Catholic Church, the communion of saints, the forgiveness of sins, the resurrection of the body, and life everlasting. Amen.

*Our Father:* Our Father, Who art in Heaven; hallowed be Thy Name; Thy kingdom come, Thy will be done on Earth as it is in Heaven. Give us this day our daily bread; and forgive us our trespasses as we forgive those who trespass against us; and lead us not into temptation, but deliver us from evil. Amen.

*Hail Mary:* Hail Mary, full of grace, the Lord is with thee; blessed art thou among women, and blessed is the fruit of thy womb, Jesus. Holy Mary, mother of God, pray for us sinners, now and at the hour of our death. Amen

*Glory Be to the Father:* Glory be to the Father, the Son, and to the Holy Spirit. As it was in the beginning, is now, and ever shall be, world without end. Amen.

*Fatima Prayer:* O my Jesus, have mercy on us. Forgive us our sins, save us from the fires of hell, and lead all souls to Heaven, especially those who have most need of thy mercy. Amen.

*Hail, Holy Queen* (sometimes prayed before the first and last decades): Hail, Holy Queen, Mother of Mercy, our life, our sweetness, and our hope! To thee do we cry, poor banished children of Eve; to thee do we send up our sighs, mourning and weeping in this valley of tears. Turn then, most gracious advocate, thine eyes of mercy toward us and after this our exile show unto us the blessed fruit of thy womb, Jesus. O clement, O loving, O sweet Virgin Mary. Pray for us, O Holy Mother of God . . . that we may be made worthy of the promises of Christ.

Let us pray: O God, whose only-begotten Son, by his life, death, and resurrection has purchased for us the rewards of eternal life, grant, we beseech you, that meditating on the Mysteries of the most holy Rosary of the Blessed Virgin Mary, we may both imitate what they contain and obtain what they promise, through the same Christ our Lord. Amen.

*Act of Contrition* [use any of the following]: O my God, I am heartily sorry for having offended Thee, and I detest all my sins because of Thy just punishments, but most of all because they offend Thee, my God, Who art all-good and deserving of all my love. I firmly resolve, with the help of Thy grace, to sin no more and to avoid the near occasions of sin. Amen.

O my God, I am sorry for my sins with all my heart. In choosing to do wrong and failing to do good, I have sinned against You, Whom I should love above all things. I firmly intend, with Your help, to do penance, to sin no more, and to avoid whatever leads me to sin. Our Savior Jesus Christ suffered and died for us. In his name, my God, have mercy. Amen.

O my God, I am sorry for my sins because I have offended You. I know I should love You above all things. Help me to do penance, to do better, and to avoid anything that might lead me to sin. Amen.

### The Official Way to Pray the Rosary

1.  While holding the cross/crucifix, make the *Sign of the Cross* and then recite the *Apostles' Creed*.

2.  Recite the *Our Father* on the first large bead.

3.  On each of the three small beads, recite a *Hail Mary*.

4.  Recite the *Glory Be to the Father* and the *Fatima Prayer* in between the three beads of the *Hail Mary* and the next large bead.

5. On the large bead, recall the first Rosary Mystery and recite the *Our Father*. The Joyful Mysteries are meditated on Monday and Saturday, Sundays of Advent, and after Epiphany until Lent. The Sorrowful Mysteries are meditated on Tuesday and Friday, and Sundays in Lent. The Glorious Mysteries are meditated on Wednesday and Sunday. The Luminous Mysteries are meditated on Thursday.

6. On each of the adjacent ten small beads (also referred to as a decade) recite a *Hail Mary* while reflecting on the Mystery.

7. In between the decade and the next large bead, recite the *Glory Be to the Father* and the *Fatima Prayer*. (Here, you may also say the *Act of Contrition*.)

8. On the large bead, say the *Our Father*.

9. Each succeeding decade is prayed in a similar manner by recalling the appropriate Mystery, reciting the *Our Father,* ten *Hail Mary*s, the *Glory Be to the Father,* the *Fatima Prayer,* and the *Act of Contrition*.

10. When the fifth Mystery is completed, the Rosary is usually concluded with another prayer called *Hail, Holy Queen.*

### Benefits of Praying the Rosary

1. It gradually give us a perfect knowledge of Jesus Christ.

2. It purifies our souls, washing away sin.

3. It gives us victory over all our enemies.

4. It makes it easy for us to practice virtue.

5. It sets us on fire with love for our Lord.

6. It enriches us with graces and merits.

7. It supplies us with what is needed to pay all our debts to God and to our fellow humans; and finally, it obtains all kinds of graces for us from Almighty God.

## Blessings of the Rosary

1. Sinners are forgiven.

2. Souls that thirst are refreshed.

3. Those who are fettered have their bonds broken.

4. Those who weep find happiness.

5. Those who are tempted find peace.

6. The poor find help.

7. The religious are reformed.

8. Those who are ignorant are instructed.

9. The living learn to overcome pride.

10. The dead (the Holy Souls) have their pains eased by suffrages.

## The 15 Promises of the Virgin Mary

1.  Whoever shall faithfully serve me by the recitation of the Rosary, shall receive signal graces.

2.  I promise my special protection and the greatest graces to all those who shall recite the Rosary.

3.  The Rosary shall be a powerful armor against hell; it will destroy vice, decrease sin, and defeat heresies.

4.  It will cause virtue and good works to flourish; it will obtain for souls the abundant mercy of God; it will withdraw the hearts of people from the love of the world and its vanities, and will lift them to the desire of eternal things. Oh, that souls would sanctify themselves by this means.

5.  The soul that recommends itself to me by the recitation of the Rosary shall not perish.

6.  Whoever shall recite the Rosary devoutly, applying himself to the consideration of these Sacred Mysteries, shall never be conquered by

misfortune. God will not chastise him in His justice, he shall not perish by an unprovided death; if he be just, he shall remain in the grace of God and become worthy of eternal life.

7. Whoever shall have a true devotion for the Rosary shall not die without the Sacraments of the Church.

8. Those who are faithful to recite the Rosary shall have, during their life and at their death, the light of God and the plentitude of His graces; at the moment of death they shall participate in the merits of the Saints in Paradise.

9. I shall deliver from purgatory those who have been devoted to the Rosary.

10. The faithful children of the Rosary shall merit a high degree of glory in Heaven.

11. You shall obtain all you ask of me by the recitation of the Rosary.

12. All those who propagate the Holy Rosary shall be aided by me in their necessities.

13. I have obtained from my Divine son that all the advocates of the Rosary shall have for intercessors the entire celestial court during their life and at the hour of their death.

14. All who recite the Rosary are my children, and brothers and sisters of my only son, Jesus Christ.

15. Devotion of my Rosary is a great sign of predestination.

## The Five Joyful Mysteries

### Monday and Saturday:

1. The Annunciation
2. The Visitation
3. The Birth of Jesus
4. The Presentation
5. Finding of the Child Jesus in the Temple

## The Five Luminous Mysteries

### Thursday:

1. Christ's Baptism in the Jordan
2. Christ's Self-Revelation at the Wedding of Cana
3. Christ's Proclamation of the Kingdom of God
4. Christ's Transfiguration
5. Christ's Institution of the Eucharist

## The Five Sorrowful Mysteries

### Tuesday and Friday:

1. The Agony in the Garden
2. The Scourging at the Pillar
3. The Crowning with Thorns
4. The Carrying of the Cross
5. The Crucifixion

## The Five Glorious Mysteries

### Wednesday and Sunday:

1. The Resurrection
2. The Ascension
3. The Descent of the Holy Spirit
4. The Assumption
5. The Coronation

❧❦

# Chapter Four

# *Practical Praying:*
## *Creating Your Story*

This section of the book is to be used as a writing journal, and is designed for you to track your progress. I want you to be able to explore your thoughts and capture them along your journey of . . . *believing, creating,* and *achieving!*

## Your Own Personal Discovery

"Discovery" happens for people at various times in their

lives. Some people go through most of their existence never giving a second thought to the possibility of the existence of a Higher Power. For others, a deep-rooted faith in God, an afterlife, or some form of Universal Life Force is taught or adopted as fact at a young age.

I believe that each one of us from time to time has that desperate moment when we call upon a Higher Power—be it God or the spiritual energy of family and friends who've crossed over—for assistance and guidance. I personally have a different perspective on prayer because of the 20 years I've spent working as a psychic medium communicating with people who are very much alive on the Other Side, even though many of their living family members and friends might refer to them as "dead."

Anyway, my advice is not to wait until your car is out of gas and running on fumes before you pull over to top off your spiritual gas tank. Incorporating prayer into your daily life ensures that you'll never be caught running on (spiritual) empty on a lonely road with no one to turn to for help. Prayer is an energy that I believe acts as a catalyst in our lives to increase our productivity, enhance our personal fulfillment, and assist us in acquiring the life lessons we're put on this planet to learn.

Take a moment right now and contemplate a problem or challenge you've experienced, one that you perhaps turned to a Higher Power to help resolve. Reflect on it for a moment, then write it down. What was the outcome?

_____

_____

_____

_____

_____

_____

_____

_____

_____

_____

_____

_____

_____

_____

_____

_____

_____

_____

_____

_____

_____

_____

Now, think about a life crisis or situation that you would have loved, or maybe still would love, to have assistance with. Share it here:

_____

_____

_____

_____

_____

_____

_____

_____

_____

_____

_____

_____

_____

_____

_____

_____

_____

_____

_____

Are you finding it difficult to pick just one? Did more than one situation jump into your mind? I wouldn't be at all surprised if you could think of many instances where, in hindsight, you realized that a little extra help or spiritual assistance might have made things better.

Going through life without prayer can be a bleak, even desperate, experience. It's like living in a dark pit your entire life, not knowing that sunshine and fresh air are only a foot away if you could just call out for help from above.

Discovering prayer is a very powerful experience—many times it's introduced or found at a time of deep conflict. Take a moment and contemplate why you're reading this book right now: Are you having that *discovery* now (or maybe it's a *re-discovery*)?

Write down what areas of your life you'd like to spiritually fuel up or illuminate from this point forward. Try to summarize in a few sentences what your goals would be if you learned to harness and utilize the power of prayer, starting today. How would you change your life? What would you want to achieve?

_____

_____

_____

_____

_____

_____

_____

_____

_____

_____

_____

_____

_____

_____

_____

_____

_____

_____

_____

_____

_____

_____

_____

_____

Again, probably quite a few areas in your life came to mind, and I'm sure that a number of them revolve around cash and material goods. Let's face it: Money and finances are subjects that many of us view as a source of conflict and unhappiness. *If I only had a little more money, I'd be able to do this or that,* we think. *I'd be happy, I'd be fulfilled, I'd be loved.* But would we?

Yes, it's true, money can help us buy many creature comforts and make some surface issues in our lives much easier to deal with. But the truly important matters, the core issues of the soul, the self, and the spirit, cannot be fixed or repaired no matter how much money we may amass.

In my private practice, I've seen a number of clients who blame everything that's negative in their lives on the simple fact that they have little or no financial security. For most of them, I agree that having a bit extra would make their current situations easier. Yet if they were to receive anything more than "enough," those same people would start living beyond their means and quickly find themselves right back in the same unhappy place they were in before. It's all relative.

For example, an attractive woman came to me for a session, and I could clearly see that there was immense negativity surrounding her life, particularly in her marriage. The average person would look at this woman and think that she had absolutely everything going for her: lots of friends, plenty of money, a gorgeous home, good looks, exquisite jewelry, and the finest clothes. She's the type of person you wouldn't find riding the subway or flying coach—she's first class all the way. But even when she was smiling, I could tell that she was miserable. To the outside world she appeared to have everything, but inside she was running on empty, because she had no spiritual connection to anything or anyone.

Every time she tried to talk to her husband about her feelings and the state of their marriage, he shut her out emotionally and showered her with more trinkets. Now, while that *did* do the trick for many years, in the end they got divorced.

I'm happy to report that she finally found the strength to walk away from everything that she once thought would bring her contentment. When I saw her a couple of years later, she'd traded in her designer clothes for jeans and T-shirts, and had adopted an attitude that was beyond radiant. She'd given up millions of dollars for something truly priceless . . . herself. In that process, she became more spiritual, got healthier, and even developed a sense of humor. In other words, she gave up the mansion to put her spiritual house in order.

I only share her story here because materially she had it all, but that couldn't buy her happiness—it merely numbed her pain. Now, I'm sure some of you are thinking, *Poor little rich girl, her diamond shoes were too tight . . . I wouldn't mind having my pain numbed like that!*

All I can say is if you're supposed to be "numbed like that" or be on that path in this lifetime, you'll have the opportunity to make that happen. But let's say that it's not your path—you aren't going to have the mansion, yacht, butler, and maid; and people won't address you as Mr. or Mrs. Trump. So be it! Money isn't the way to truly *enrich* your life—I honestly believe that the greatest riches in this lifetime are to be found through prayer.

This is a central theme that I can't stress often enough: This is a book about utilizing prayer to enrich and enhance your life, not to find a way to buy it. So please don't pray for that Mercedes, yacht, diamond ring, private island, or lottery jackpot; instead, concentrate on areas of your inner self. And be selfless in your intentions by praying for others as well as yourself. Utilize prayer as an energy force that can bring clarity and focus into your life. Remember, praying with intent is an extension of yourself and your own energy—whatever you project out into the universe will be brought right back home to you, so be careful what you pray for.

The process of incorporating practical praying into your routine may not bring you wealth, but it might very well bring you something more important—*abundance* . . . in all areas. That is, if you can achieve betterment in all aspects and areas of your life, and you're putting passion into your life, profession, and direction, then profit will be achieved in many areas.

## Your Spiritual Journey

At this point in your life, you've probably either recently discovered prayer, or you're having the "discovery" right now. This discovery is your first step on your lifelong spiritual journey.

The concept of "the journey" is important, because it's really synonymous with your life. How we travel is just as important as where we end up. The choices we make in life ripple out and around us like waves from a pebble tossed into a pond. Many people stand back and watch the experience from the shore. But by honoring the journey, you not only become part of the pebble, but part of the water, the ripples, the shore, and the sky. You become part of the bigger picture in its entirety. The journey you're undertaking—discovering and embracing prayer, God, and Spirit into your life—is an introspective experience. Many people in your life may start seeing a significant difference in you and not fully understand what it is.

Take a moment to think of people in your life whom you'd feel safe and comfortable sharing your spiritual thoughts with. Write down their names.

_____

_____

_____

Now list the people you're sure you *wouldn't* be comfortable discussing spiritual issues with:

_____

_____

_____

_____

_____

_____

_____

_____

_____

_____

_____

_____

I hope that you don't think me overly pessimistic for leaving more lines for you to write down the names of people with whom you would *not* feel comfortable discussing your spiritual journey. But I'm sure that in time, the many names on the DND (do not discuss) list will begin to shift to the list of "spiritual confidants."

## Beginning the Prayer Dialogue

This is the most challenging part of the book, because it's the place where many of you might feel foolish. If you haven't prayed for years, or you only do so from time to time, you might feel as if you don't deserve to have your own personal dialogue with God. But the real beauty of this process is that the Prayer Dialogue erases that feeling very quickly.

Take a moment and do this quick meditation [please refer to the CD]:

- Take six long, deep inhaling breaths by *slowly* breathing in through your nose and then *slowly* exhaling through your mouth.

- Visualize a place that makes you feel relaxed and peaceful: It might be a tranquil beach, park, or meadow . . . maybe even an empty church.

- Continue your meditative breathing as we go on.

- Imagine two very large, gentle hands opening in the sky above you.

- Visualize a white and gold light beginning to emanate from the center of each palm. The warmth of the colors and light shower over you.

- Take a moment to slowly breathe in this light.

- Repeat in your mind or out loud: "I encircle myself in the White Light of God's Universal Love and Divine Protection."

- Now visualize the hands coming down around you. . . . Step inside . . . and imagine yourself reclining into these hands . . . all the while being bathed in the white and gold light. Now slowly take three deep, cleansing breaths.

- Repeat in your mind or out loud: "From this day on, I want to begin my prayer journey by creating my own Prayer Dialogue. . . . "

- Visualize the following colors emanating upward from the palms: red . . . orange . . . yellow . . . green . . . blue . . . purple . . . white. Slowly breathe in and exhale at least once with each color. Feel yourself being bathed in the warmth of the color and light.

- Slowly take three more deep, cleansing breaths.

Know that from this point forward, you've embarked on creating your own Prayer Dialogue. The important thing is to maintain it. Write in a journal to keep track of your experiences. Record what you were able to visualize and how it made you feel. If you had a difficult time visualizing some portion of this, jot that down. Don't worry if you had a tough time with any part of this process; it takes time and practice.

## How to Pray Practically

The process of practical praying is simple. It means that you'll take each decade of the Rosary and apply your intention toward it. As I said earlier, "intention" means that you'll aim, or target, your prayers for a particular purpose. The Rosary is divided into five different decades, and that means that every time you begin to pray, you have five intentions to direct your prayer energy toward.

When praying the Rosary in the official way, you're directed to meditate on the life of Christ; while in the process of practical praying, you're meditating on aspects of your own life or the world, and directing the prayer energy toward that end. (Some people who are familiar with the official version of praying the Rosary can do both, which is why I've also included the official method.)

By thinking about prayer energy as a laser beam—that is, something that you can direct—you can aim it toward a situation like peace in the Middle East, or more personally toward a loved one who might be going through a tough time emotionally or physically. The possibilities are endless.

Let's begin.

### Beginning Prayers

- Begin by blessing yourself—you can use the *Sign of the Cross* to start
- Say the *Lord's Prayer (Our Father)*
- Say three *Hail Mary*s
- Say *Glory Be to the Father*
- And then say one *Our Father*

## First Decade

**Intention:**
I'm praying this decade for [state your personal intentions here]:

_____

_____

_____

_____

_____

_____

_____

_____

While you pray this decade, meditate on your purpose by saying:

- Ten *Hail Mary*s
- One *Fatima Prayer*
- And one *Our Father*

## Second Decade

**Intention:**
I'm praying this decade for [state your personal intentions here]:

_____

_____

_____

_____

_____

_____

_____

_____

While you pray this decade, meditate on your purpose by saying:

- Ten *Hail Mary*s
- One *Fatima Prayer*
- And one *Our Father*

## Third Decade

**Intention:**
I'm praying this decade for [state your personal intentions here]:

_____

_____

_____

_____

_____

_____

_____

_____

While you pray this decade, meditate on your purpose by saying:

- Ten *Hail Mary*s
- One *Fatima Prayer*
- And one *Our Father*

## Fourth Decade

**Intention:**
I'm praying this decade for [state your personal intentions here]:

_____

_____

_____

_____

_____

_____

_____

_____

While you pray this decade, meditate on your purpose by saying:

- Ten *Hail Mary*s
- One *Fatima Prayer*
- And one *Our Father*

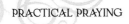

## Fifth Decade

**Intention:**
I'm praying this decade for [state your personal intentions here]:

_____

_____

_____

_____

_____

_____

_____

_____

While you pray this decade, meditate on your purpose by saying:

- Ten *Hail Marys*
- One *Fatima Prayer*
- And one *Our Father*

## Ending

Reflect on all five intentions and begin the wrap-up of this prayer session:

- One *Glory Be to the Father*
- One *Fatima Prayer*
- One *Our Father*
- Three *Hail Mary*s
- One *Our Father*
- Bless yourself to end . . . with the *Sign of the Cross*

You've now completed a session of practical praying. Please feel free to adapt this process to your own method of prayer. Remember, as I stated earlier, prayer is a personal journey. My intention with this book is to get you to start the Prayer Dialogue and incorporate more prayer into your life, and if you so desire, the Rosary could be a tool to assist you.

I hope that you've found this book helpful and enjoyable.

≈◦≈

# Reference

*Introduction:*

[1] Definition of *meditation* from
**www.encyclopediabritannica.com**

[2] Definition of *Rosary* from **www.encyclopedia.com**

[3] Definition of *prayer* from **www.religioustolerance.org**

*Chapter 3:*

Information on praying the official way comes from
**www.theholyrosary.org** and **www.sancta.org**

For more information on the official prayer of the Rosary, you
can write to: Crown of Thorns, P.O. Box 49, Lingfield, Surrey RH7
6YQ, England

# About the Author

**John Edward** is an internationally acclaimed psychic medium, and author of the *New York Times* bestsellers *One Last Time, Crossing Over, What If God Were the Sun?, After Life,* and *Final Beginnings*. In addition to hosting his own syndicated television show, *Crossing Over with John Edward,* John has been a frequent guest on *Larry King Live* and many other talk shows, and was featured in the HBO documentary *Life After Life.* He publishes his own newsletter and also conducts workshops and seminars around the country. John lives in New York with his family.

For more information, see John's
Website: **www.johnedward.net**.

# Prayer Notes

# Prayer Notes

# Prayer Notes

# Prayer Notes

# Prayer Notes

# Prayer Notes

# Prayer Notes

# Prayer Notes

# Prayer Notes

# Prayer Notes

*P*

We hope you enjoyed this Princess Books publication.
If you would like more information about Princess Books,
you may contact the company through their distributor, Hay House, Inc.:

Hay House, Inc.
P.O. Box 5100
Carlsbad, CA 92018-5100

**(760) 431-7695** or **(800) 654-5126**
**(760) 431-6948 (fax)** or **(800) 650-5115 (fax)**
**www.hayhouse.com**

∞◦◦

*Distributed in Australia by:*
Hay House Australia Pty. Ltd., • 18/36 Ralph St. • Alexandria NSW 2015 • *Phone:* 612-9669-4299 • *Fax:* 612-9669-4144 • www.hayhouse.com.au

*Distributed in the United Kingdom by:*
Hay House UK, Ltd. • Unit 62, Canalot Studios • 222 Kensal Rd., London W10 5BN • *Phone:* 44-20-8962-1230 • *Fax:* 44-20-8962-1239 • www.hayhouse.co.uk

*Distributed in the Republic of South Africa by:*
Hay House SA (Pty), Ltd., P.O. Box 990, Witkoppen 2068
• *Phone/Fax:* 27-11-706-6612 • orders@psdprom.co.za

*Distributed in Canada by:*
Raincoast • 9050 Shaughnessy St., Vancouver, B.C. V6P 6E5
• *Phone:* (604) 323-7100 • *Fax:* (604) 323-2600

∞◦◦

Tune in to **www.hayhouseradio.com**™ for the best in inspirational talk radio featuring top Hay House authors!
And, sign up via the Hay House USA Website to receive the Hay House online newsletter and stay informed about what's going on with your favorite authors. You'll receive bimonthly announcements about: Discounts and Offers, Special Events, Product Highlights, Free Excerpts, Giveaways, and more!
**www.hayhouse.com**